ISBN: 979-8-9851094-4-3

Design by: Taja Ferguson, Yasir Nadeem

The Trauma in Transition
by Dr. Christopher E. Dodd

This book is written in honor of Doshia and E.C. Dodd and their legacy of love.

Acknowledgements

As I ponder the completion of my first published book, I'm reminded of the African Proverb, "If you want to go fast, go alone. If you want to go far, go together." My vision for this book has only been realized because of the sensational people within my sphere of influence. Thank you to my family Schlonda and the three Presidents (Kennedi, Raygan and Madison) for allowing me to invest my time, talent, and treasure into this project. Thank you to my dream team—Rachel, Tonia, Keith, Bianca, and Marcie. I'm grateful for your tireless work on this project. Thank you to my New Community family, mentors, and friends who provided vital feedback. Your kindness will never be forgotten. Finally, thank you to my parents who instilled in me that all things are possible to those who believe. I love you and miss you. I close with the quote, "Faith makes things possible—not easy." May this book serve to illustrate that no trauma can overwhelm those who are willing to trust in God to guide us to our purpose and promise.

Introduction

I have an open door policy. All are welcome, whether they are seeking spiritual advice or simply a listening ear. Part of that is because I am a pastor with a divine calling to oversee my congregation. The other part is who I am as a Myers-Briggs branded extreme extrovert. And if the end of the day rolls around and I have received no visitors, the sentiment still stands. An open door means an open invitation.

It was a few days after Christmas when I discovered that I had been locked out of my own office. Members of the board had changed the locks behind my back in an effort to drive me from the church. My secretary at the time was my goddaughter, and they even did her the favor of boxing up her belongings and leaving them in the hall like an evicted tenant who had not paid her rent.

This violation of trust should not have surprised me. I was a new leader in a deeply fractured community where I had never been entirely welcome. My predecessor was beloved by the congregation and his exit was abrupt, leaving no room to grieve his absence. Attendance was dwindling, tensions were high, and I was to blame for it all.

Prior to the lockout, my critics produced a list of all of my infractions. They delivered it to me in the form of an eleven-page document on Christmas Eve and told me I would be taking a sabbatical, whether I liked it or not.

"O Come, All Ye Faithful... Except for you. Yeah, you. We don't want you here."

They were finally shutting me out. The new lock on my office door made my forced sabbatical official. Furthermore, it was a symbol of the pain I endured from a volatile leadership changeover. All of the toxic behavior and emotional baggage culminated in this ugly act of retaliation. There would be many more damaging moments to come. People I cared for would turn on me. My sphere of influence would beg me to consider other opportunities, even to the point of relocation. I would be in more pain than I knew how to bear.

It took the intervention of a friend, a Passionate Peter if you will, to literally kick the door down. I got my office back, but it was never quite the same after the incident. There were days I would just stare at my door. It was difficult to get anything done with this painful reminder only feet away from me. I was heartbroken. No longer was my office a place of comfort for myself and others. Who knew when they would try to evict us again? Was my place here even worth salvaging? What did God have to say about any of this?

When I talk about this part of my life with others, I call it a transition. And when I reflect on the lasting effects that this transition had on me—emotionally, spiritually, socially—and the organization I lead, I call it trauma.

Transition is more than a wait-and-see from point A to point B. It marks an evolution. It is inescapable, regardless of your race, gender, age, net worth, or spiritual enlightenment. At some juncture along the path of life, we all travel on the Trauma Train and derail at the boulevard called "Change, Or Else." Transitions are especially impactful for those of us in leadership positions, with the weight of our followers' futures to carry in addition to our own. And when there is conflict at every turn, trauma is unavoidable.

As the leader of an organization, I had to learn from the trauma in transition in order to take care of myself and the people God called me to shepherd. In this book, I recount my own experiences, as well as those of both scriptural and secular leaders in the face of adversity. In the first chapter, I outline for you the ways in which trauma can manifest from leadership transitions, centering on the acknowledgement and reframing of painful encounters. Next, you and I will examine the pieces of a broken organization, defining our strengths and weaknesses as individuals and team players with measurable assessments. After that, we will seek the partnerships needed to navigate such transitions in qualified professionals and our own social circles. Then, we will work together to establish rituals and routines that will heal our spirits, bodies, and relationships. At the end of our time together, we will hone in on the mindset needed to maintain forward momentum toward God's vision for you and your organization.

Consider this message from Revelation 3:8 NIV—

> "I know your deeds. See, I have placed before you an open door that no one can shut. I know that you have little strength, yet you have kept my word and have not denied my name."

Despite my difficulties, I have found that all of the important doors—the ones that lead to my ultimate, God-given purpose—keep opening. That is not to say that there are no challenges behind them. But for as long as I have kept an open door policy for my congregation, God has kept the door open for me.

Before we begin, a prayer:

Father, in the name of Jesus, we come to you to help us navigate our broken hearts and communities. Let us rise above adversity, learning from the trauma in transition to catalyze growth on a personal level that will ultimately benefit those we are called to lead.

Bless us as we move forward in you. In Jesus' name, amen.

Chapter 1

The Pain in Transition

Let's Get Ready to Rumble

In the 1982 film *Rocky III*, titular character Rocky Balboa begins as the Heavyweight Champion of the World. After successfully defending his title and gaining newfound popularity and wealth as the Italian Stallion, Rocky finds himself on the radar of hungry title contender Clubber Lang, played by Hollywood's favorite tough guy of the '80s, Mr. T.

Rocky and Lang face off twice in the film, the first fight a bitter loss for Rocky and the second a climactic rematch. In a locker room interview, a correspondent asks Lang to share his prediction for the fight. The outspoken champion usually expresses himself in several biting words, but in this memorable moment he responds with a one-word answer: "Pain."

World movers and shakers—people at the apex of their industry—are not exempt from heartache, sacrifice, and adversity. Even Steve Jobs, co-founder of Apple, was forced out of his own company for a span of twelve long years. Despite this, he would become one of the greatest inspirational figures in the modern technology industry, developing the Apple products we know and love today. For Rocky and Clubber, vying for the championship title is pursuing the greatest opportunity of a fighter's career. Pain is the one unavoidable outcome, regardless of the winner. In other words, great opportunity invites the possibility of great pain.

The opposite can be true as well, with the right perspective. People of influence often tell stories of the storms they weathered in order to become who they are now. It was Franklin D. Roosevelt who said, "A smooth sea never made a skilled sailor." Enduring great pain can serve as a catalyst for personal growth and development, an opportunity for betterment in and of itself. Just like Rocky, to reach one's full potential is to win the fight of your life.

Change of Plans

In the words of Iron Mike Tyson, "Everyone has a plan until they get punched in the mouth!" I had a plan when the small congregation I had nurtured in a high school gym joined with my predecessor's church, forming the congregation I lead to this day. Together, the two communities would forge a strong foundation for racial reconciliation and community transformation in the south suburbs of Cook County. The church is situated in a predominantly African American neighborhood and, at the time of transition, we were hemorrhaging white attendees.

In 2013, I was the first African American Lead Pastor in the 125-year history of the church, as well as the first senior leader to be voted into the position rather than simply promoted. In a "get to know the new guy" meeting, one of the longtime Caucasian members of the congregation asked me how I would champion racial reconciliation. In response, I half-jokingly asked the board if they would help me bus the white people back into the neighborhood now that the great exodus had already begun.

Let's just say they did not like that response.

Still, my Doctoral studies in Christian Community Development and my thesis topic on socioeconomic reconciliation suited their vision. My ascension into a senior position was made possible by a nearly unanimous vote. Excitement outweighed any concern for potential conflict in the future and I ignored the warning signs.

Shortly after the honeymoon period of becoming the new Lead Pastor, I experienced a series of one-two punches to the mouth over the course of five years. It began with small character assassinations, then escalated to outbursts in front of the congregation. In each and every toxic meeting I was sucker punched with some new complaint about my style of preaching, my new ideas, my personality—*one-two, one-two, one-two!*

I could have submitted to the bullying and nonconstructive criticism. I could have thrown in the towel and accepted defeat. Maybe my life would have been easier had I picked up my family and relocated to a new church. But herein lies the challenge of leadership: Growing as a leader is allowing what you learn from painful experiences to alter your course of action. As Denzel Washington's character says in *The Equalizer 2*, "There are two kinds of pain in this world. The pain that hurts, the pain that alters."

In this chapter, I will describe pain in its many forms: emotional, physical, spiritual, and social. I will also touch on the pain that infiltrates an organization as a whole, infecting members with low morale. Recognizing each kind of pain, analyzing its origins, and anticipating the struggle to come can help us heal ourselves. Only then will we be empowered to guide our fractured communities down the road of recovery with us.

Emotional Pain

First, an excerpt from Genesis 37 NIV:

> "Joseph had a dream, and when he told it to his brothers, they hated him all the more.
>
> He said to them, 'Listen to this dream I had:

We were binding sheaves of grain out in the field when suddenly my sheaf rose and stood upright, while your sheaves gathered around mine and bowed down to it.'

His brothers said to him, 'Do you intend to reign over us? Will you actually rule us?' And they hated him all the more because of his dream and what he had said."

Joseph was an interpreter of dreams, and these dreams he had as a young man were prophecies of his future as the ruler of Egypt. But his brothers, fueled by their jealousy and hate, threw him into a reservoir and sold him into slavery. Can you imagine the trauma of being betrayed by the very people you are looking to for support? To be forsaken by one's family is to experience great emotional pain.

Family is not always blood, and we as churchgoers often refer to one another as brothers and sisters in Christ. This solidifies our relationships in our Father's house, creating a shared vulnerability. But with enough hurtful words and actions, what happens to our understanding of "family" when it seems all we do is inflict pain on each other?

Emotional pain cannot be ignored, but it can be shoved down deep inside. When it is suppressed, this kind of pain is irritating at best. Critics may feel inclined to unload their verbal and written abuse on you, and we as the Lord's shepherds must respond in a Christ-like manner, never returning the favor. As much as we might like to lash out with our own profanity-laced retaliation, we cannot stoop to that level. It is a voluntary suppression of one's own voice. This is what I call emotional waterboarding—the constant drip of negativity onto a self-imposed gag, causing a slow suffocation.

If you are anything like me, hurtful words seep below the surface until you are sinking in an ocean of negativity. Though you may return to some semblance of normalcy, the pain remains the way wet clothes stick to your skin. Suddenly, everything and everyone irritates you. Those against you wish to drag you down. Those with you cannot understand.

Emotional pain unchecked can be very damaging to our sense of security. When we experience great emotional hurt, we humans tend to build fences around our hearts so that no one else can harm us and, likewise, we cannot harm anyone else. This self-inflicted solitary confinement breeds cynicism about the intentions of those around you. Like the story of the injured lion, even those who try to help by removing the thorn from the lion's paw run the risk of getting the claws.

Though I am a proud extrovert, I began to prefer isolation. No one could hurt me if I kept them at arm's length. Meanwhile, Joseph's story is one of reconciliation with his family—of forgiveness of past wrongs against him. He was the prototype for Jesus in this way, a man whose response to great adversity paved a path to ultimate forgiveness. How we as victims of emotional pain evolve into Judicious Josephs is vital to our journey through the trauma in transition. How we control that pain and handle it maturely determines the fate of our followers too.

Physical Pain

If you have ever stubbed your toe then you know what it is like to be incapacitated with pain, even for just a moment. Certain physical traumas can knock the wind out of you and leave you tiptoeing through life, afraid to feel that kind of pain again. We know that a physically painful experience can yield an emotional response like fear or frustration, but what about vice versa?

Studies show that unchecked emotional baggage can negatively affect your physical health. Dr. Elizabeth Hartney, former writer of online resource *Verywell Mind*, lists digestive issues, headaches, dizziness, nausea and even muscle pain as being connected to emotional distress. According to Hartney, emotional and physical pain may not be as independent of each other as experts once thought; rather, they are connected on a neurological level.

So, what does one do when emotional distress becomes physical pain? Coping with an emotion-based physical condition is not as simple as taking a day off to recover from a cold. Physical pain borne of emotional distress is relentless, making it difficult to focus on one's work. Chronic medical conditions that cause great physical pain require short or long term disability insurance plans. However, as church leaders with a divine calling to oversee our congregations, we must have a regular presence in the church. Sick days and sabbaticals are all well and good, but the common church-goer will perceive their pastor as a symbol of God's constancy in their own life. When it affects your performance at work as well as the efficacy of your symbolic presence in the church, you know you have a problem.

In my own experience coping with emotional pain, I struggled with loss of appetite and increased anxiety. I slept poorly at night and dealt with fatigue throughout the day. Eventually, I learned to eat something and sneak a quick nap prior to every meeting, preparing for a fight that would require all of my energy. While the emotional pain I endured from those meetings would still cause me physical pain, recognizing my symptoms as a result of distress helped me exercise control over my own well-being.

Spiritual Pain

Let us first remember Psalm 13:1 NIV:

"How long, LORD? Will you forget me forever? How long will you hide your face from me?"

—and Matthew 27:46 NIV:

"About three in the afternoon Jesus cried out in a loud voice, 'Eli, Eli, lema sabachthani?' which means 'My God, my God, why have you forsaken me?'"

In a moment of great pain, even our Savior asks why he has been forsaken by the Almighty. It is only natural for church leaders to question our assignment under the weight of traumatic experiences. When the pain feels unbearable, we turn skyward and point fingers at God.

What did I do to deserve this? Have you forgotten about me?

We see an example of this doubt in the Lord with the Apostle Peter later in the Gospel of Matthew. After Jesus is taken into custody by the authorities, Peter is in clear and present danger of being discovered as a disciple of Christ. When confronted, Peter denies Jesus not once, not twice, but three times. In his fear that God would not protect him, Peter denounces the Son in order to protect himself.

In this series of events, Peter was undergoing a great transition, yanked from the security of being a follower of Christ and dragged directly into the line of fire for his discipleship. These breaking points are common when our faith is challenged. My own spiritual pain resulted in daily pity parties before God. Instead of placing my trust in the Lord, I wanted a way out. I hired a professional to update my resume. I networked with churches from out of state. I was willing and eager to relocate my family and flee from these constant trials of faith.

It is within these trials, however, that God does His best work. The saying goes, "When God closes a door, he opens a window." We must appreciate how God redirects us, for it is when we are running away from our problems that He reorients us and places us back on the path toward true reliance on Him.

Social Pain

Perhaps metaphors of closed doors and opened windows do not inspire you, having witnessed your critics on the other side of that door turning the key in the lock. God may be in control, but humans are unpredictable and unfair in their actions. Instead, maybe these familiar lyrics may resonate with you:

> "How do I say goodbye to what we had?
> The good times that made us laugh
> Outweigh the bad
> I thought we'd get to see forever
> But forever's gone away
> It's so hard to say goodbye to yesterday…"

"It's So Hard to Say Goodbye to Yesterday" was a chart-topping single in 1991 originally written by husband and wife Freddie Perren and Christine Yarian, remixed by Boyz II Men. The song speaks to anyone who has mourned the loss of a relationship, be it through the finality of death or an irreconcilable disagreement in life.

It is a hurtful and heart-wrenching experience to watch people leave your organization. Furthermore, as pastors, God has called us to reach out to the lost, and our position demands that we keep a close eye on our flock. But how can you complete your work within God's vision if members of the congregation want nothing to do with you? There is nothing worse than standing at the pulpit every Sunday morning and watching a once full sanctuary dwindle to half its size.

No matter the method of departure, it is distressing to lose a lamb you have been called to shepherd. People in a church community will go about their departure in different ways. In an exit interview an individual may say that your approach to leadership is the problem, or worse, your very personality. How do you respond to judgments like that? Others may credit their decision to the movement of the Spirit, saying that God is pushing them to serve elsewhere. How can you argue with the Spirit?

The emotional chart topper of departures is when people leave without any communication. You do your pastoral duty of reaching out only to have your phone calls and letters met with radio silence. These are the people for whom you officiated weddings and funerals. The people you visited in the hospital when they were weak and sick or when they gave birth to their children. The people in your heart and on your mind to this day. It is an incredibly difficult task to accept a departure like this without taking the motivation personally, especially when the reasons are usually among these:

A. "I'm leaving because I have a problem with your leadership."
B. "I'm leaving because I have a problem with your personality."
C. "I'm leaving because the spirit is moving me elsewhere."
D. " . . . " (Subtext: "I don't want to talk to you.")

Since you are the common denominator among three of the four options, your thoughts may become consumed with insecurities.

Am I driving people away? Should I change who I am to better accommodate others? Why do people keep misunderstanding me? Is this all my fault?

Try asking yourself those questions without spiraling into a complete identity crisis. In the next chapter, we will further elaborate on the difficulties of people-pleasing and how to be your authentic self in the face of self-doubt. But first, we must examine the effects social pain can have on a larger scale when a whole organization is involved in a traumatic transition.

Organizational Pain

"A great war leaves a country with three armies: an army of cripples, an army of mourners, and an army of thieves."

— German Proverb

A shell-shocked country will wade through years of fallout after a devastating event. In addition to your own hurt as the leader of an organization, you will witness how pain infiltrates your followers as a whole through loss of morale, members, and money.

When there is a sudden change in leadership, the organization must be given a chance to grieve the loss of the old ways before abiding by the new norms. Grief is classically spoken of in terms of five steps: Denial, Anger, Bargaining, Depression, and Acceptance. When one or more of these steps are skipped, stalled, or stayed, discontent brews. If I have learned anything from attending therapy these last several years, it is that grief is messy. It is rarely as cut and dry as one linear path from Denial to Acceptance.

Members of your organization may still be stuck in the messy middle of grief. This breeds low morale, manifesting as poor communication, excessive complaining, and heightened tensions. In the case of my church community, the first symptom arose from inconsistency in our method of communication—board meetings were too aggressive while emails were too passive. The second made itself known through strange accusations: "The music is too loud!" or, "The worship team needs a dress code!" The third and perhaps most damaging symptom of low morale was the tension, rising high above the church steeple.

Despite our motto proclaiming love for both God and people, we did not love each other. We could barely coexist in a ninety-minute church service together. Solutions felt unattainable; after all, it becomes extremely difficult to address major problems when no one wants to come to the table to solve them. No one even wants to come to the building. In my own church community, this was seen in rows upon rows of empty seats. Even those meant to be the most spiritually mature in the congregation—the elder board—would come to church to teach their Sunday school classes and leave before morning worship.

Low morale has a high price tag. Gallup, an analytics and advisory company based in Washington, D.C., provides interesting insight on the financial effect of low morale. They estimate that there are 22 million actively disengaged employees in America, costing our economy as much as $300 billion per year in lost productivity. When your organization loses morale, it loses member retention and positivity, and before long, funds deplete. Just like a corporation cannot run without investors, a church cannot run without offerings.

The Pie Chart of Pain

In this chapter, we explored the impact pain can have on different aspects of life—emotionally, physically, spiritually, socially—and your organization. Each of these "slices" contribute to the greater trauma of a sticky transition. In the next chapter, we will further examine the broken pieces, focusing on their origins and your response to pain moving forward. But first, I encourage you to take a few moments to apply this reading to your own experiences. Allow the below questions to prompt this reflection.

1. Was there ever a time in your life when a difficult transition had a traumatic impact on you? How would you describe that experience?

2. How has trauma affected you emotionally, physically, spiritually, and socially? How has trauma affected the organization you lead?

3. How has this chapter challenged you to see trauma from a different perspective?

Chapter 2

The Pieces of the Puzzle

Some Assembly Required

Imagine a rainy afternoon. An hour has passed since you dumped all the necessary pieces of the jigsaw puzzle out of the box. You were so confident in your choice of family activity, but by now, you and your puzzling team should have finished. Instead, there is barely a border on this piecemealed scene. Colorful piles, each unofficially titled *sky*, *grass*, *clouds*, and so on, are the only evidence of your progress. The room is silent besides your defeated sighs and the ticking of the clock overhead. You would rather not know what time it is, knowing deep down that barely a minute has passed since you last snuck a glance.

Just when it feels hopeless, you finally hit your stride. Pieces are snapping together like, well, like pieces in a puzzle should, and the picture is becoming clearer and clearer with each connection. But then, if you somehow manage to finish the puzzle, you are frustrated to discover that a piece is missing. Those under the age of twelve start crying. Those over the age of twelve are a breath away from spewing profanities. Who suggested a puzzle anyways?

My wife is the patient one in the family. I am more likely to set the box on fire than live to see the final picture. Maybe I'm not a "puzzle person" like some, but I can appreciate the practice of working together to create a bigger picture. Similarly, when people come together—each with their own jagged edges—they do so for a greater purpose. Just like every piece has its place in the puzzle, every member of your organization has their own role.

Now imagine before you a five-hundred-piece puzzle, complete and perfect in its design. When your organization is functioning exactly how it should be, it will look like this. Now imagine that your leadership team makes up the pieces along the border, maintaining the structure and integrity of the organization from all sides. The most important pieces of that border are the corners—the cornerstones, if you will. Each corner piece symbolizes a vital duty of your work as the visionary in charge. I use the acronym LEAD:

1. **L**earn
2. **E**mpower
3. **A**nticipate
4. **D**edicate

In this chapter I will elaborate on each of these cornerstones for strong leadership. Each will serve as guidelines for the leader who is traversing the trauma in transition, wondering how best to rediscover that harmonious functionality within their organization.

Learn and Lead from Your Strengths

Anyone who has ever been interviewed has heard these two questions: *What are your strengths? What are your weaknesses?* Each of us is uniquely wired to approach our environment in the way suited best to our talents, experiences, and preferences. Chances are, if you have made it so far in life that you are a leader of an organization, you are no stranger to yourself. But as we all grow and change, it is beneficial to revisit those interview questions introspectively. Years ago, in the midst of my most traumatic experiences, I took an assessment based on the Myers-Briggs Type Indicator, a commonly used personality test that categorizes people into sixteen distinct personality types. These sixteen types are combinations of four basic preferences:

Favorite World: ***Extraversion*** or ***Introversion***
Information: ***Sensing*** or ***Intuition***
Decisions: ***Thinking*** or ***Feeling***
Structure: ***Judging*** or ***Perceiving***

Utilizing the first letter of each preference, the test assigns you a personality type. Based on my results, I am an ESFJ, described as, "Warmhearted, conscientious, and cooperative." The designation goes on to say that I will work hard to establish a harmonious working environment, surrounding myself with those who will hold me accountable for completing projects in an accurate and timely manner. It also says that I am loyal to others and intuitive of their needs, appreciating their talents the same way I wish to be appreciated.

Reading my Myers-Briggs Type for the first time was an astonishing experience as it felt so true to who I am. Does this description encapsulate me one hundred percent of the time? Not necessarily. Does it help me understand why I think and act the way that I do compared to the other people in my life? Absolutely. The Myers-Briggs Type Indicator has given me clarity, empowering me to develop my personal strengths while still acknowledging my weaknesses.

It's important to note that no one type is superior to another. According to The Myers & Briggs Foundation, "All types are equal: The goal of knowing about personality type is to understand and appreciate differences between people. As all types are equal, there is no best type."

Correspondingly, there is no one right leadership style. For example, I personally thrive in a fast-paced, harmonious working environment filled with rich conversation. My predecessor, on the other hand, was introverted. He preferred to problem-solve alone in his office. He was a strategic genius, a man with a plan for every aspect of ministry. I will not speculate what his specific Myers-Briggs type was. All I know is that we are very different people, and stepping into his uniquely tailored shoes was setting myself up for failure.

I felt much like David in 1 Samuel 17:38-39 NIV:

"Then Saul dressed David in his own tunic. He put a coat of armor on him and a bronze helmet on his head. David fastened on his sword over the tunic and tried walking around, because he was not used to them.

'I cannot go in these,' he said to Saul, 'because I am not used to them.' So he took them off."

The best advice I can give you as you navigate a leadership transition is simple: Don't wear someone else's armor. Your predecessor likely had their own way of doing things, a way that suited them and their personal strengths. You are not the same person as them. You have already collected the pieces of your own armor over the years of your leadership tenure—a breastplate from captaining your high school basketball team; gauntlets from your first promotion to a managerial position; a helmet made of the providential gifts that allow you to command a room.

It will be a challenge not to mimic the previous leader, but authenticity is necessary in order to thrive in your position. If you attempt to emulate a leadership style that does not come naturally to you, your conformity will conflict with your instincts, tearing holes in your work ethic and the organization's overall progression.

Take Matthew 9:17 NIV:

"Neither do people pour new wine into old wineskins. If they do, the skins will burst; the wine will run out and the wineskins will be ruined. No, they pour new wine into new wineskins, and both are preserved."

Your leadership style is unique to you, as divinely designed as the microscopic cells in your body. This is not to say that you should not seek and accept advice from your predecessors; rather you should allow their wisdom and lived experience to inform your own approach in the way that makes the most sense for you.

In the words of the great writer Oscar Wilde, "Be yourself; everyone else is taken."

Empower Others to Operate in their Strengths

By now you may have noticed that I often choose to preface my own words with the wise words of others—an intentional gesture I will speak more on in this section. In that spirit, there is an old African proverb that states, "If you want to go fast, go alone. If you want to go far, go together." As leaders, we know that true progress is impossible without a core group of people acting in roles of support. Without a team that both respects and responds, a leader is at a severe disadvantage, making decisions in a vacuum that is not representative of their community.

Who, then, belongs on the team? If you have the privilege of assigning your own team, your first impulse may be to surround yourself with people who think and function just like you. This approach, however, does not breed the results you may expect. A room of Chris Dodds, for example, would resemble some mashup of stand-up comedy and talk therapy. People would leave feeling better, but was anything accomplished?

Rather than working in an echo chamber, you must surround yourself with people who will better you. Confucius states, "If you're the smartest person in the room, you're in the wrong room." It takes a humble leader to invite those with more intelligence into the decision-making room. The expert opinions and lived experiences of other people in the room stretches understanding and facilitates new perspectives.

As a leader, you run the risk of sucking all the air out of any room you're in. It may be a challenge to listen and learn if you are accustomed to total control. Whether you have assigned your own team or stepped into an already cemented group, your ultimate purpose as the leader in the room is to encourage and empower those around you. Each member of your team has their own prime space of maximized potential; it is just a matter of spending the time to listen to their individual needs.

Consider these examples. Those who are most productive when in direct contact with others may not deliver if sequestered to a cubicle. Meanwhile, a post-meeting outing may not be attainable for someone whose energy tank needs to refuel between long meetings. Someone who is easily overwhelmed by the big picture may be best suited in a detail-oriented capacity, focusing on logistics that are gradually checked off a to-do list. Likewise, someone who is frustrated by the details may prefer to paint with broader strokes.

Truth be told, administration sucks the life out of me. That's why I delegate the fine-tuning to those better equipped to sort through the nuances.

Without the right tools, discovering everyone's prime space of maximized potential may be an arduous process involving hours of exhausting interviews and group discussions. This is why I recommend that all teams, no matter how large or small, use the DiSC Profile—a personal assessment tool used to improve team dynamics and productivity. Like the Myers-Briggs Type Indicator, the DiSC Profile requires users to answer a questionnaire that measures four qualities:

Dominance (D)
influence (i)

Steadiness (S)
Conscientiousness (C)

My results revealed my predominant quality to be "influence (i)"—
summarized as being "motivated by social recognition, group
activities, and relationships. [i styles] prioritize taking action,
collaboration, and expressing enthusiasm and are often described as
warm, trusting, optimistic, magnetic, enthusiastic, and convincing."

The full DiSC Profile goes on to describe how I can best relate to
the others who received different results than me; how to orchestrate
my own leadership style to enhance my effectiveness in various
situations; how to curate my natural responses to conflict to be most
productive; and much, much more.

Other members of my team have taken the assessment, receiving
different results tailored to their unique personalities. As a whole,
the Profile has allowed us to objectively evaluate our teamwork,
communication tactics, and productivity. My colleague with the
most "Conscientiousness (C)" finds her maximum potential in
detail-oriented projects like crafting the annual budget. Another
colleague with the most "Steadiness (S)" finds his maximum
potential when his introversion is accommodated with projects he
can do alone on his own time.

It is important to note that everyone has levels of each quality within
them; your Profile is not a case of binaries like the Myers-Briggs
Type Indicator. My capacity to "influence (I)" is simply higher than
that of my colleague, just as her "Conscientiousness (C)" is more
impactful than mine. No one Profile is better or worse than another;
rather it is when each Profile is respected in their own right that the
organization itself becomes better.

Anticipate Conflict and Articulate Vision

We cannot discuss the betterment of an organization without recognizing the inevitable. If you put a group of people in a room—each with their own Myers-Briggs type and DiSC Profile—and ask them to solve a problem, disagreements will naturally ensue. Sometimes disagreements yield a more refined, thorough solution, simply assisting the overall critical thinking process. Other times, disagreements evolve into full-blown conflicts. In my experience, the vast majority of conflicts stem from misunderstanding. Let us reflect on the words of one of my favorite authors:

> "As dynamic leaders, we will be misunderstood. No matter how much innovation and energy we bring to our assignments, there will be those in our ecosystems who will think we're moving at warp speed and they can't keep up. Or they might be standing in places where their view is limited or dark, and they can't see what we're doing."

— Dr. Joseph W. Walker, *Leadership & Loneliness*

Notice that Walker puts the blame on neither party, because there is no one to blame. To be misunderstood is simply an unavoidable rite of passage for those of us in leadership positions. In the words of Nelson Mandela, "It is also the fate of leadership to be misunderstood." People will think of you as prideful, arrogant, overly ambitious. You will be called a disrupter, a pot-stirrer. The traditionalists will have deep nostalgia for the way things were before you came into the picture, and you will be blamed for every bump in the road between past and present. There will be glorification of the old ways and fixation on the flaws of today—namely, *your* flaws.

You must realize that when you are misunderstood, you are in great company. Ralph Waldo Emerson wrote, "Is it so bad, then, to be misunderstood? Pythagoras was misunderstood, and Socrates, and Jesus, and Luther, and Copernicus, and Galileo, and Newton, and every pure and wise spirit that ever took flesh. To be great is to be misunderstood." We who have chosen the path of the leader will always upset the status quo in the name of progress because, to paraphrase a familiar saying, we can spend our whole lives in the comfort zone, but it would be foolish to expect anything to grow there.

How then do you address and move on from the misunderstanding? I recommend the writings of Dr. Walker, quoted above, on this matter. He offers helpful tips and reminders to best address misunderstanding within your organization, emphasizing the calm and consistent articulation of your decisions. To properly clarify your position, it is vital that your decision be directly tied to the vision of the organization—a reminder, even, of the reason why you were given the position you currently hold. There is a reason you are here; as long as you are crystal clear in that area, you will be able to articulate the intentions behind your decisions.

A vision is not quite the same as a mission. According to leadership specialist Thomas Griffin, "Mission statements give meaning to the actions of your organization right now. They are present-oriented… Vision statements, on the other hand, give meaning to the actions of your organization in the future. They are future-oriented." The connection between the two are the actions needed to see your mission materialize into your vision. As a formula, this relationship would look like this: mission + actions = vision

It was the vision of my church to be a multiethnic community, where people of all colors felt welcome. Our mission was centered on the love of our Heavenly Father and all of his children—it still is to this day. In order to actualize our mission-led vision, my studies in socioeconomic reconciliation would arm me with the tools needed to tear down the walls between the haves and have-nots.

The church, situated in a predominantly African American community, began hemorrhaging white members with the departure of my predecessor. Having brought with me a small

African American congregation of my own via the merge, I was blamed for the leaks in the boat, often accused of throwing members overboard with my leadership style. Every time we hit a choppy wave, my critics would scrutinize my decisions, searching for any intentions contradictory to the church's mission or their personal preferences. These investigations would yield misunderstandings of my character, which would then metastasize into dramatic conflicts.

One misunderstanding resulted from the decision of the elder board to invest in the cost of my doctoral studies, all the while voicing their misgivings around my area of study. If I were to break down this particular instance, it would look something like this:

The Issue: Pastor Chris is studying the philosophy of Christian Community Development.
The Assumption: His doctoral studies are not based in the tenets of discipleship.
The Misunderstanding: Pastor Chris is using church money for his own personal gain.

My life as a bivocational provider—both the student and the teacher—would endure repeated hyper-examination. My critics questioned my experience, my dissertation, even the price of my car. Years after gaining the title I would continually need to prove myself worthy, all the while providing for my three daughters and wife. In response, I articulated the following:

The Truth: I am studying the very issue this church faces.
The Personal Vision: I want to create socioeconomic reconciliation within our congregation.
The Organizational Vision: Socioeconomic reconciliation (the action) will produce a multi-ethnic congregation (the vision) in line with our motto of loving God and people (the mission).

The original misunderstanding seems so easily clarified with a breakdown as reasonable as this. The unfortunate truth of the matter is that some people are not reasonable. Some people will not be responsive to your explanations, even if your choices are rooted in the mission of the organization. In my case, such people believed that my area of study was not Biblical enough for them, simply because it centered on real world application rather than theological ideals. When reason meets rebuttal, it is more important than ever to rely on God as the compass for your safe passage through the trauma in transition.

Dedicate and Refuse to Detour from God's Vision

Imagine before you a dark road with only the occasional street light to illuminate the way. The voice on your phone's navigating system has long since quieted after giving you a vague command to continue onward, miles and miles ago. You begin to question your whereabouts, squinting along the side of the road for mile markers, signs, any indication that you are where you are supposed to be. You turn down the music, as if that will help you see any better. An hour passes; the road is dark and isolating. It is getting harder and harder to trust the directions you so confidently relied on in the daylight.

Just because God is providing the road before you does not mean that you will be exempt from challenges along the way. Detours are inevitable, provoked by real world obstacles and the ensuing doubt in God's plan for you. Let us refer to Mark 4:35-40 NIV:

> "When that evening came, He said to His disciples, 'Let us cross to the other side.'
> After they had dismissed the crowd, they took Jesus with them, since He was already in the boat. And there were other boats with Him.
> Soon a violent windstorm came up, and the waves were breaking over the boat, so that it was being swamped. But Jesus was in the stern, sleeping on the cushion. So they woke Him and said, 'Teacher, don't you care that we are

perishing?'
Then Jesus got up and rebuked the wind and the sea.
'Silence!' He commanded. 'Be still!' And the wind died
down, and it was perfectly calm.
'Why are you so afraid?' He asked. 'Do you still have no
faith?'"

Faith in Christ is the ultimate compass. In life you will inevitably
detour from the northward point of the needle. It is how you
dedicate yourself to Him, despite the detour, that determines your
fate. By following a reroute inspired by fear, you are certain to end
up in no man's land. Take Jonah, for instance, who defied the
Lord's wishes so dramatically that he ended up in the belly of a
whale. But by following a reroute inspired by trust in God's
omnipotence, you will end up like Joseph, the young man who
turned his poverty into prosperity.

We as leaders must trust in God's plan for us, remaining hyper-
vigilant of the signs that our community is still on the right path.
Take for example the institutionalized gatekeeping that inhibits the
growth of the Body of Christ. At my church, holier-than-thou
judgments plagued the community, from the top of the food chain
to the very bottom. If any prospective church member was deemed
unfit (a.k.a., a sinner) by an elder, they could be denied acceptance
into the church body. This was in direct opposition to my own
personal philosophy of evangelism—it's tough to clean a fish before
you catch it.

It took years of gradual changes and the self-righteous exits of
certain modern-day Pharisees before we were able to reintroduce
the mercy of God within our walls. During that time, I oscillated
between doubting myself and doubting God. It was when I circled
back to the point at which I lost my way and returned the path God
set for me that I could hear His voice again. The equation is simple:
If we expect our followers to trust in us, then we as leaders must
trust in God.

To close this section, I offer my life's scripture, Proverbs 3:5-6 NIV:

> "Trust in the LORD with all your heart,
> and lean not on your own understanding;
> in all your ways acknowledge Him,
> and He will make your paths straight."

The Big Picture

The puzzle of your organization will not be perfect. There will be flaws—perhaps a few pieces missing or worn down from years of being crammed in the wrong place. The border may not be complete yet and the corners might need some work. Similarly, your congregation may have dwindled, or you may not have your ideal leadership team yet. But by learning your strengths and empowering others in theirs; by addressing conflict with a vision and mission in mind; and by trusting in God, your organization will come together amidst the trauma in transition.

In the next chapter, we will explore the different practices you can implement in your life to better yourself on an individual level. Before we get personal, take a moment to answer the following questions.

1. Sit down with a spouse, friend, or trusted coworker. Ask them, "What are my three greatest strengths?" Tell them their greatest strengths in return.

2. How often do you find yourself operating in your strengths? If you struggle to operate in your strengths, what adjustments to your core team do you need to make in order to maximize effectiveness?

3. Describe a time when you were misunderstood and your character questioned. How did you attempt to clarify your position? If you did not successfully clarify your position at the time, how would you do it now after reading this chapter?

Chapter 3

Partnerships for Progress

"A pinch of this and a pinch of that."

My father never told me how to season his beloved barbecue before he passed. He was an excellent griller, knowing just the right proportions and timing to cook a meal so delicious that it makes my mouth water just to remember it. At every barbecue, he would prepare food like he was feeding a small army, even though there were only three of us. When friends of the family attended, it was common for folks to carry home aluminum-covered paper plates filled with steak, ribs, and chicken. Our fridge was always brimming for weeks after.

Losing my father and my mother within twenty-three days of each other was a special kind of traumatic experience. To this day I still try to recreate my dad's grilling recipe. I get closer and closer to the right flavors every time I grill out with my own family. I think my dad would be proud of me for continuing the tradition and focusing on what truly matters: community.

The following are my recommendations for a well-rounded community, but just like a unique family recipe, your version may be heavier on some ingredients and lighter on others. Let this serve as a starting point for you to observe and understand the roles of those around you. Then, consider where there may be a lack of support and how you might supplement your life with newfound relationships.

Mental Health Professionals

What is your understanding of conditions like depression and anxiety? Mine has developed deeply over the last several years. I learned that depression is not the same as sadness, nor is it quite like mourning. It is a permeating sickness that infiltrates your thoughts, whispering in your ear, "Wouldn't it be easier if you just gave up on this painful thing called life?" Anxiety, meanwhile, is more than nerves before a big interview. It consumes and controls, revealing a world so vicious that nothing feels safe anymore. It grips you tight and causes sleepless nights.

Combating mental illnesses and emotional hardships is not as easy as praying the rain clouds away. In my experience, it requires consistent therapy with a mental health professional, as well as the desire to make a lasting change. Some people even require prescribed medications to supplement their healing journey. While that was not my personal experience, I support those who do rely on medication to treat their chemical imbalances.

Therapy has been an important fixture in my life for years. My denomination affiliation, Converge Worldwide, graciously sponsors ten therapy sessions a year for pastors and their families. The program is family-oriented, because when one person is experiencing hardship of the mind, it inevitably affects those around them. My family was certainly suffering from my bitter moods and emotional exhaustion. In the most traumatic moments of my leadership transition, my survival instincts inspired an entrance into the world of mental health. I asked God, "Does this make me a bad Christian? If my faith does not erase my pain, am I fit to lead others in Christ?"

This is the stigma among the faith community around mental healthcare. If a follower of Christ is struggling with depression or anxiety, any solution but prayer is looked down upon. It is as if you are not a real Christian if you cannot trust in God to lift the fog of depression or clear the storms of anxiety. It is without question that God answers prayers. He is Our Heavenly Father and we should not doubt His plan for each of us. However, God also expects us to take care of ourselves.

Take the story of the prophet Elijah in 1 Kings. In the wake of death threats from Jezebel, Elijah runs away and hides in the wilderness. 1 Kings 19:4 NIV says—

> "He came to a broom bush, sat down under it and prayed that he might die. 'I have had enough, LORD,' he said. 'Take my life; I am no better than my ancestors.'"

God answers his prayer, sending an angel with food and water and commanding him to take care of himself by seeking the support of other rulers and prophets. We see God provide Elijah with a support system—Hazael, Jehu, and Elisha—if only he would lift his downcast eyes and see.

Just like with Elijah, God provides each of us with the people we need when we need them. It was God who inspired the mental health professionals of the world onto the healing journey they now lead others on. These are individuals who are best suited to assist you in times of need, offering insight on the inner workings of your mind and advice on your next course of action.

When I placed my trust in God and the resources He put before me, I found solace in therapy. It activated a pressure release valve inside of me, freeing me of my deepest frustrations and hurts. With so many unhealthy vices I could have fallen into—alcohol consumption, self-medicating, couch-potato escapism, to name a few—I found a healthy alternative that actually helped me process my trauma instead of ignoring it.

Healthy does not mean easy. Therapy is by no means a walk in the park. Finding a therapist is a struggle on its own. Just because someone has the title does not mean that they will be the right match for you and your specific needs. During this time you will learn whether you prefer in-person sessions or online video calls, or a combination of both. There is a "dating" period in which you will seek out a meaningful connection with different therapists, eventually committing to the one that you feel most comfortable opening up to.

"Comfort"—that is another source of emotional stagnation for some. If you cannot be emotionally naked with your therapist, there is only so much they can do for you. Vulnerability is a necessity when the subject at hand is the head or the heart. When the impulse to retreat back into your protective shell arises, trust in the science of psychology and keep in mind that God has put this person in your life for a reason.

Mentors

This next partnership is one you might recognize. The mentors in your life are the people who are equipped to give you perspective and personal examples of overcoming difficulty through trying times. Since there is no rule stating that you can only have one mentor in your lifetime, I recommend at least one mentor per focus: family life, work life, and personal life. Rather than leaning heavily on one individual who can provide an all-knowing comprehensive mentorship, I rely on a collection of sages. This collection is part-organic—loved ones who have grown into mentors over time; and part-curated—individuals I have sought out based on their area of study or experience.

My mother was a mentor to me, and her "lead by example" mentality lingers with me to this day. It was through my mother that my devotion to God flourished, ever since the days she dragged me to Lilydale Progressive Missionary Baptist Church when I was a reluctant child who would much rather spend his time watching professional wrestling every Sunday morning. She wanted me to have a faith-based background, enrolling me in Christian schools and emphasizing God's presence in my life from day one. I owe my career in ministry to her.

Another mentor of mine is an advisor from seminary, Dr. Gerald Dew. When I was completing my doctoral degree, there were many attempts of assassination against my character. Needing someone to validate my plan to fight fire with fire, I sought the advice of Dr. Dew. Instead of pandering to my anger, he said, "Don't wrestle with pigs. You both get filthy and the pigs like it." This humorous but powerful visual has come to mind every time I feel resentment overpowering my Christ-like sensibilities, reminding me to stay calm and collected.

I am lucky to have a mentorship with one of my colleagues as well. During this last year of surviving the covid-19 pandemic, the wisdom of Pastor Andrew Singleton shines like a lighthouse in a storm. With his background as a certified public accountant, he has been instrumental in the development of a fiscal recovery plan, advising me on the steps our church must take to stay above water. I also value him as a dear friend.

Just as you can find mentors within your family and friends, you will discover them in your favorite autobiographies and memoirs. I often return to the writings of John C. Maxwell in his book *Sometimes You Win—Sometimes You Learn.* As one of my personal favorite authors and leadership mentors, I learned through his teachings that I could improve everything around me by improving myself. This has been a pinnacle of my own personal success, and the reason I am able to write this book after years of self-examination and improvement.

Maxwell, Pastor Andrew, Dr. Dew, and even my mother are all leaders just like me. These are the most meaningful mentorships I could ask for. While none of them claim to have the exact same experiences as I do, they are able to empathize with my pain from a personal place.

I promise that if you look around, you will notice the people in your own life who have acted as mentors to you. They are the guiding lights that illuminate the way before you when it is too dark to anticipate what will come next. They are the people who are willing to share their scars and advise you on how to avoid racking up your own.

Coaches

A coach is different from a mentor and equally valuable to the decision-making part of your life. While a mentor can offer you advice that informs your choices, a coach will help you formulate a game plan. In other words, coaches are action-based, whereas mentors are philosophy-based. A game plan crafted by your coach will be complete with action items rooted in proven methods of problem-solving that you can implement over time to better yourself.

Similar to mentors, you will have several coaches over the course of your life, specializing in a variety of fields—finances, career, parenting, etc. You can expect these life coaches to take different approaches to their instruction based on their personality and priorities. One coach might be in your face, knocking some sense into you like Mike Ditka. Another might be the kind that puts their arm around your shoulders and points the way like Tony Dungy.

Your coach must know you for your unique talents and capabilities. Magic Johnson, for example, had a flourishing career as a basketball player. When he coached the Lakers in 1994, he became frustrated that his players did not have the same skills on the court as he did. When you are the best, it is difficult to drag others up to your expert level. After all, a brilliant athlete does not always make for a brilliant coach. Your coach should be able to see your talents and help you craft the best plan of action based on your skills and your needs.

Some of my coaches came into my life as early as grammar school. My band teacher would not let me quit playing the trumpet, even when I thought my braces would come blasting out the other end of the instrument. Instead, he supervised my experimentation with other instruments, encouraging me to continue nurturing my musical talents.

Another coach in my life was my basketball coach in seventh and eighth grade. When I became cocky and complacent in the starting lineup, Coach benched me until I could once again appreciate the significance of my place. On the bench, watching my teammates, I rediscovered my hunger to play and play well. It was not until I recognized the honor of a spot on the starting lineup that I was allowed on the court again.

At present, I am honored to be a coach for others. I have learned that it is best not to project my own talents and skills onto those looking to me for help, expecting them to handle a situation the way I would. My children, for instance, are not a perfect DNA copy of me—they share DNA with their mother, who is different from me in many wonderful ways. Recognizing this, I am able to coach each of them through life with a personalized approach catered to their unique personalities.

The coaches in your life ultimately want the best for you, even if that means instilling some good, old-fashioned humility. Trust in their intimate knowledge of you and you will be better equipped to formulate a game plan that will allow you to stick to your strengths.

Accountability Partners

Is there someone in your life who knows you better than anyone else? This could be your spouse, your sibling, or even your best friend. The ones who know the good, the bad, and the ugly are your accountability partners. This kind of partnership is honest and blunt, sharing a mutual concern for each other when the going gets tough.

Sometimes, the pressures of transition can force you into a position where you are no longer being true to yourself. An accountability partner knows you so well that when you are not acting like yourself, they can sense it. Sometimes, we do not want to hear what they have to say. We do not want to acknowledge the effects of the pain we are in for fear that we might finally have to confront it. Facing our flaws with the help of a friend, however, is the safest and most effective way to overcome them.

We need those who are willing to dwell in our pain with us, to be physically present in some of life's most difficult moments. As we know, pain can be terribly isolating, as if one is travelling down a dark and winding path with no clear destination in sight. However, with a partner there with you, you no longer need to carry all of that pain alone.

Recall the covenant of friendship between David and Jonathan in 1 Samuel 18:3-4 NIV—

> "Then Jonathan made a covenant with David because he loved him as himself. And Jonathan removed the robe he was wearing and gave it to David, along with his tunic, his sword, his bow, and his belt."

And then again in 1 Samuel 20:13-17 NIV when Jonathan says the following—

> "'May the Lord be with you as He has been with my father. But show me unfailing kindness like the Lord's kindness as long as I live, so that I may not be killed, and do not ever cut off your kindness from my family—not even when the Lord has cut off every one of David's enemies from the face of the earth.'
>
> So Jonathan made a covenant with the house of David, saying, 'May the Lord call David's enemies to account.' And

Jonathan had David reaffirm his oath out of love for him, because he loved him as he loved himself."

David and Jonathan's friendship is frequently referenced as the ideal partnership between equals. Jonathan gives David the clothes off of his back, overflowing with support for David. In return, David vows to protect and care for Jonathan's family.

Accountability partnerships are rooted in deep and abiding friendship. Unlike mental health professionals, mentors, and coaches, you must play an equal role in this partnership. It is an equivalent exchange between individuals who care intimately for one another. When your accountability partner is in need, it is your turn to support them. It is a seasonal but equal relationship between kindred spirits.

Tribes

Proverbs 13:20 NIV states—

"Walk with the wise and become wise, for a companion of fools suffers harm."

The people we spend the most time with—in laughter or in tears—are those that have a direct and lasting effect on our lives. This group partnership is best described as a tribe. Because of their close and constant proximity, your tribe is as critical to the healing journey through the trauma in transition as any mental health professional, mentor, coach, or accountability partner.

Your tribe can be your family, your colleagues, your closest friends. They are the people who innately know the right way to support you. They know how to offer solutions that you will respond to. They know when to speak and when to be silent. Most importantly, they know how to love you without being selfish. Your tribe will laugh alongside you in times of celebration and hold you close in times of trouble.

Leaning on your tribe is a sign of strength. Sometimes I find myself in a worry spiral, forgetting to communicate my needs to those who love me the most. It is then that I remember the lyrics of the Whodini song "Friends"—

> "Friends—how many of us have them?
> Friends—ones we can depend on?
> Friends—how many of us have them?
> Friends. Before we go any further, let's be
> Friends."

When you are stuck in the muck of trauma, you will need your tribe more than ever to pull you out of the quicksand and back on sturdy land. Your health and happiness are of top priority to your tribe. While an accountability partner is focused on keeping you true to your best self, your tribe is loyal even at your worst. Their support is unwavering, to the point of offering to drop-kick whoever hurt you. You are each others' ride or die. When you need them, they are there. And when they need you, you are there.

The Family Recipe

Each kind of partnership I have discovered in my life represents a key ingredient in my ultimate success. Talking with my therapist has offered a sense of release. Deferring to the wisdom of my mentors has informed my decisions. Collaborating with my coaches has kept me moving on the path of progress. Listening to my accountability partners has kept me true to myself and true to those I love. Leaning on my tribe when I need support has given me the safety and reassurance I need at my lowest points.

These partnerships are often right in front of you, waiting to be recognized and valued for their unique offerings. Trust in God to provide the proper ingredients for the family recipe—then do your part to honor and savor them.

The next chapter will challenge you to explore the practices necessary to navigate the trauma in transition. These routines and rituals can be spiritual, physical, and even recreational. Before we continue, consider answering the following questions about the partnerships in your life.

1. What are your current anxieties in regards to seeking help from a mental health professional? How does the stigma against mental health professionals affect your personal opinion of that kind of partnership?

2. List three partners—a mentor, a coach, and an accountability partner—in your life that would aid your healing journey, if only you would allow them into your head and heart.

3. As you assess your sphere of influence, who are the people in your tribe? Who are you vulnerable with? Who is vulnerable with you? How does vulnerability make you closer to one another?

Chapter 4

Practices for Progress

I would like to open this next chapter with a change of pace. Normally, I ask you questions at the end, first giving you the context needed to gather your thoughts. But if you're an overachiever like I am, reading this book from start to finish, you need breaks built into the process to truly digest the content. We see these breaks in all sorts of activities—in basketball, you have half-time; during a theatrical performance, intermission; at school, recess. At this point in the book, allow me to press pause on our trajectory so you can check in with yourself. Respond to these questions at your leisure and remember: there are no wrong answers.

What time did you wake up this morning?

What was your energy level—high, low, somewhere in between? How about now?

Considering this energy level, what are you excited about? What is troubling you?

Are you experiencing any anxiety today? If so, where does this anxiety manifest in your life—is it spiritual, emotional, social, financial? Somewhere else?

What obstacles against your happiness did you encounter today?

What obstacles against your happiness do you anticipate encountering tomorrow?

What are you seeking to learn today? Tomorrow?

How have you witnessed improvement in your life?

How will you continue to foster your personal growth?

I ask you these questions to draw you further into the mindset of introspection. In this chapter, we will discuss the daily practices needed to progress through a traumatic transition, further defined as rituals and routines. As you read, I challenge you to think about your own life—what practices qualify as ritual? What habits have become routine? What sorts of rituals and routines can you implement, day to day, to activate the healing process?

And now, for some context...

Ritual, Routine, and Everything in Between

Ritual and routine are parasynonymous words, meaning they are often used interchangeably despite having different definitions in different contexts. In this case, the two terms carry different weight. Through ritual, actions that may seem arbitrary now gain deeper meaning. Take communion, for example. Sharing bread and wine at church on Sunday is only profound because of the scriptural significance assigned to it—Jesus broke bread and poured wine for his disciples, offering each as a symbol of remembrance and promise. Rituals are not exclusive to institutions like the faith community, although our religion is characterized by many. Rituals can be completed by the individual in the form of daily actions that focus the mind on reflection, ultimately promoting emotional, physical, spiritual, and social wellness.

Routines, on the other hand, are more preoccupied with maintenance than meaning. Brushing your teeth and flossing regularly are routines. So is brewing your morning cup of coffee, breaking for lunch, or turning on the TV at the end of a very long day. If rituals are the symbolic practices of life, routines are the practical operations. They are equally important in that they require you to slow down and focus on yourself.

If you do not choose to slow down, burnout will force you, defined as "an extended period of stress that feels as though it cannot be ameliorated" by Psychology Today. In other words, burnout occurs when stress levels are so high that there is no relief to be found, no improvement within sight. Burnout is what you find at the end of your rope.

My burnout was a result of the worst chapters of my traumatic transition, when my energy was at an all time low. Although this kind of stress is most commonly associated with work, its effects can extend to one's home life. I would attend my daughters' games to cheer for them, secretly wishing they would lose so I could go home and go to bed. I would forget something my wife had just said at the dinner table, physically present but mentally elsewhere.

If you're reading this book, you likely can relate to that feeling of having nothing left to give. To recover from burnout, you must take the time to heal. As we know, healing comes at a price. No longer are you improvising your day to day, trying to outrun your worst memories and tendencies with a busy schedule and no capacity for personal growth. You are allowing yourself to be still, to block out the distractions and just *be* with yourself. Now the intensity of your trauma can finally catch up to you and sneak past your shoddy defenses. Painful flashbacks hit you like shin splints of the soul and the distractions of a busy, mindless lifestyle may seem more appealing than ever.

Why dwell in the pain when you can push through and save all that awful inner work for later? The way I see it, we only hurt ourselves more the longer we wait to heal our wounds. In order to endure the trauma in transition, we need rituals and routines to remind us of what matters in life, all the while maintaining the healing process with simple, repeatable measures. My recommendation is to seek out such practices that are spiritual, physical, and recreational—practices that I believe realign us with our purpose.

Genesis to Revelation

As a devout follower of Christ and leader in the faith community, I am the first to recommend daily scripture reading. My own ritual takes up only fifteen minutes of my morning. I begin by reading the *Zondervan NIV Men's Devotional Bible* or the *YouVersion Bible App* on my phone. Then, I spend a few additional minutes reflecting on the reading in my journal and building upon my relationship with God through prayer. Your own devotional practices may differ from mine based on your needs, so consider this a framework for crafting your own unique meditation.

To begin, create an environment of solitude. Find a quiet space in your home where you can be alone with your thoughts. If that means you must wake up before the rest of your family, so be it. Carving that fifteen minutes out of life may seem easier said than done, especially for those of us with children, jobs, and countless other commitments. The truth is that it is not easy at all. In my case, being a high-energy extrovert, I struggle to embrace the quiet moments. It is difficult to steady my mind, to allow the thoughts I have repressed for so long to come to the surface. Some days, I would prefer to just fast forward through my day instead of pressing pause.

Practice makes perfect, and it has taken me years of practice to perfect my spiritual solitude. Today, I rely on the structure of morning meditation to open the door to deeper reflection of my past and intention for my future. I do not accomplish this by biting off more than I can chew of the Lord's daily bread, and neither should you. Choose the passages that mean something to you. No one expects you to read Genesis to Revelation in one week, although I applaud anyone who embarks on that journey. Start small. Even five minutes a day is an accomplishment.

The Bible may seem even less accessible for those outside the faith; still, it is invaluable for its copious examples of people enduring and overcoming hardship. For a leader who is not familiar with scripture, I encourage you to use the Internet to search for the stories that are relevant to your struggle. Search "people in the Bible who were depressed" or "leaders in the Bible who endured pain" and so on. If your search turns up empty, I recommend you thumb through a study Bible or refer to daily devotionals, allowing those who have spent their careers reckoning with the Word of God to guide your reading and reflection.

The Co-Pilot's Prayer

Reading the Word of God has great merit even on its own, but growing a relationship with Him is not possible without prayer. The good news? There is no one right way to pray. Many prefer the comfort of the Lord's Prayer, turning to the template provided by Jesus Himself in the New Testament Books of Matthew and Luke—

> "Our Father, who art in heaven,
> hallowed be Thy name;
> Thy kingdom come;
> Thy will be done;
> on Earth as it is in Heaven.
> Give us this day our daily bread.
> And forgive us our trespasses,
> as we forgive those who trespass against us.
> And lead us not into temptation;
> but deliver us from evil.
> For Thine is the kingdom,
> the power and the glory,
> for ever and ever.
> Amen."

Fancy words such as these may lose meaning when one hears them every Sunday morning. Allow me to walk you through this prayer, piece by piece, and offer an interpretation to guide your understanding.

"Our Father, who art in heaven,
hallowed be thy name…"

We begin by acknowledging our mighty God, residing in Heaven above. His name in and of itself is holy, and we enter this prayer recognizing our privilege to speak it—to worship Him.

"… Thy kingdom come;
Thy will be done;
on Earth as it is in Heaven."

We then remember His control over Heaven and Earth, even when it feels that life is out of control. He is the omnipotent pilot of our mortal existence, and we are the co-pilots, ready to submit to His will.

"Give us this day our daily bread.
And forgive us our trespasses,
as we forgive those who trespass against us."

Having offered praise and submission to God, we now ask Him for providence—to protect us and provide for our daily needs, one day at a time—and then forgiveness—to give us the treatment we proffer to our neighbors, as instructed by Jesus in Mark 12:31 NIV.

"And lead us not into temptation;
but deliver us from evil."

It is here that we ask God to guide our judgements and keep us on the path of purpose by leading us away from traps and temptations that would cause us to stray into sin.

"For Thine is the kingdom,
the power and the glory,
for ever and ever.
Amen."

We conclude on the reassurance that our lives and our collective existence on this Earth are entirely in God's hands. For all the power and glory belong to Him, for all of time.

Prayer is an intimate experience between you and God, so how you approach it is up to you and your relationship with Him. Some days, when my mind seems cloudy and I cannot find the words, I rely on the Lord's Prayer to get me where I'm going. The destination is often uncertain, and doubt inevitably creeps in. *Does God actually hear my prayers? Does He even care?*

But prayer is not a one-way flight into the unknown—you calling out to God and receiving radio silence. It is a round trip, with God returning your prayers throughout life in big and small ways, if only you hold your doubting tongue long enough to listen and learn. Afterall, we were born with two ears, two eyes, and only one mouth.

Putting Pen to Paper

With its many interpretations, the Bible is not the easiest book to absorb in one sitting. If you wish to truly digest the Lord's Word, journaling is an excellent metabolizer. To those already in the practice of journaling—keep it up. To those testing it out for the first time, know that there is no right or wrong way to keep a journal. It can be done in a special notebook purchased for the intention of daily meditations, or it can be a collection of loose-leaf papers, or even documents on your computer. You can call it a diary, a logbook, even word vomit if you so choose. The name or shape it takes is inconsequential; rather, it is the time and care you devote to the page that will determine what value you receive from it.

I begin my own journal entries with a written prayer. First, I ask for wisdom and strength—two qualities I actively strive for in life since I am so often faced with difficult decisions. Then, I ask God to watch over me and my family, to bless my wife and me with the patience and fortitude it takes to raise three children. Last, since losing my parents, I vow to bring Glory to Him by honoring their legacy.

After taking the time to talk to my Heavenly Father, I continue my journaling exercise with the help of my favorite tools—The High Performance Planner, created by motivational speaker and best-selling author Brendon Burchard. Through helpful questionnaires, rating systems, and writing prompts, I can set my intentions for the future, track my ability to remain aligned to those intentions, and then reflect on my accomplishments and areas for improvement.

While a planner as involved as this one may seem intimidating to some, I find it beneficial as a person actively trying to improve himself. The Burchard Method of carefully reporting and reflecting on one's life is by no means the only path to progress. Some variation of the questions at the beginning of this chapter, with your own personal tweaks, could accomplish the same goal. The key is to not get carried away with the concept of structuring and examining every moment of your life on the page; after all, the moment we think we may have a plan, God usually reminds us that His plan takes precedence. As I like to say to my congregation, God will not give you a schedule where there is no room for Him.

Tending Your Temple

While spiritual practices nurture a rich inner life and relationship with God, physical practices improve one's relationship with their own body. As someone prone to thought spirals and unhelpful rumination, I go into my body to get out of my head—or, in other words, I enter my temple to exit my tempests.

Undergoing daily physical practices enhances my ability to catch those curveballs in life; remaining vigilant to my goals improves my follow-through in scenarios outside of the weight room. However, since we humans are uniquely and divinely made, physical health looks different for everybody and every body. Your physical practices may look vastly different from mine based on your personal goals.

My week is divided into strength training and cardio. Mondays, Wednesdays, and Fridays, I do both lifting and bodyweight exercises, zeroing in on the particular parts of my body I want to strengthen through controlled intensity. Tuesdays and Thursdays are for—you guessed it—cardio. On those days I pop in some earbuds and listen to a hip hop, R&B, or gospel playlist to motivate me as I run for two miles or bike for ten to fifteen. Lately, I have added Sunday morning to my cardio schedule. Stamina-based exercise does wonders for me when it comes to combating the stress of leading a Sunday morning service.

Goals are reflections of your ultimate intention, whether that is to improve your strength, flexibility, stamina, or all of the above. You can write out your goals in your journal and see them come to life in the form of physical routines. Identifying the goal-based routines that are right for you, i.e., attainable and in your best interest, means you are taking care of yourself and your future. You may have heard of SMART goals, coined by George T. Doran in an academic journal entitled *Management Review*. Used as a guide for goal-setting, SMART is an acronym for Specific, Measurable, Achievable, Relevant, and Time-bound. The best way to use this tool is to turn each of these qualities back on yourself in the form of a question:

Is my goal *specific*?
(Can I clearly articulate what my goal is and why I am setting it?)

Is it *measurable*?
(Can I quantify my goal in order to track my progress?)

Is it *assignable*?
(Is this goal one I can complete on my own, or should I delegate?)

Is it *relevant?*
(Does this goal align with my other goals and my life as a whole?)

Is it *time-related?*
(Can I set a deadline for the completion of this goal?)

Determining your goals is not a task you must do alone. Personal trainers exist for the purpose of helping you find the right plan and approach to physical fitness in order to achieve your goals. If a personal trainer is outside of your budget, I recommend you turn to the free, albeit less personalized, training programs available on YouTube. My favorite channel is the dynamic duo of Mr. and Mrs. Muscle, an African American married couple who guide viewers through quick, intense workouts in a series of free videos.

A personal goal of mine is to incorporate more stretching into my physical routine. You will hear every trainer, coach, and athletic-minded person swear by stretching as a method to avoid soreness and injury. Because my instinct is to go, go, go, I find it difficult to slow down long enough to stretch. Yoga is pretty much out of the question. Still, I recognize the benefit of warming up one's body for physical exertion, so it has become a goal of mine to embrace the value of a more graceful approach to physical health.

Grace—how often do you hear that word used when describing a workout? The messages we hear most are that of "pushing it to the limit" or "no pain no gain." While progress can be found at the end of those tactics, so can injury—physical and mental. So I ask you to always keep the phrase "Grace for the Race" in mind. We give our bodies and minds grace so that we may successfully complete the race, rather than overwork ourselves to the point of being too exhausted to cross that finish line. Celebrate your small successes. We're healing, after all.

Fun is Fundamental

It feels contradictory to be serious about relaxation, but I cannot emphasize enough that we all need a break every once in a while. If you run your life like a drill sergeant and do not allow any time to breathe or—Heaven forbid—*laugh*, you will experience a swift and debilitating burnout. If laughter is, as they say, medicine for the soul, then recreation is the rehabilitation plan for an overworked and overwrought spirit.

How that recreation takes shape is up to you! I am a fan of watching comedy specials, as most comedians have a history of pain that they can now look back on with a sharp sense of humor. I also enjoy plot-heavy TV dramas that pull me out of my own life and its various problems and into the dramatic lives of fictional characters. I enjoy grilling out for my family, reading books by my favorite authors, and watching sermons of great communicators.

The older you get, the harder it is to organically discover recreation. Life can fill up quick with commitments, and it often takes careful planning to set aside time for relaxation. Planning your fun does not make it any less fun. If anything, it makes the experience mean more. Date nights with my wife, UNO with the kids, NBA Playoffs with my friends—all of these activities require that I close my laptop at a certain time of day and put the work away. In a post-quarantine world that saw many of us working from home for long periods of time, planned fun is more necessary than ever.

The pursuit of recreation is just as important in the workplace as it is at home. I ask my team to submit weekly reports, answering a couple questions about their professional goals and personal interests. In addition to understanding their state of mind at work, I want to know what my teammates enjoy doing in their free time, what their interests are. As a bonus, my team gets to see life laid out right in front of them. They witness the push and pull between the personal and the professional, often in disproportion to each other.

With this exercise and the conversations it spurs in turn, I remind my team of the importance of enjoying their lives while they have them.

The Juggling Act

The rituals and routines you implement into your life will aid you in your healing journey. For some, these recommended practices may fit nicely into existing rituals and routines. Others may experience this chapter as an upheaval of life as they know it, for keeping oneself accountable to their intentions is easier said than done. Those intentions slip through the cracks caused by self-doubt and mind-numbing distractions. Those practices—spiritual, physical, or recreational—fade away, overshadowed by the brokenness of you. And broken we all are, and whole we all wish to be.

Wholeness is another word for life balance. Imagine yourself as a juggler, and each ball is labeled with a different practice for progress. One is a morning run, another a journaling exercise, the third a game night with the family. Spend too much energy on one and not the other two, and soon your juggling act comes tumbling down. Seek balance, for the key to keeping them all aloft is to touch each ball evenly, keeping a steady beat to a song in your head. Mine is the song "Total Praise" by Richard Smallwood. What is yours?

If you're looking for the end-of-chapter questions, they're at the beginning.

Chapter 5

Progressing Past Pain

I have an open door policy. If I did not, I do not know if I would have made it this far in my healing journey. Had I shut the door to the partnerships and practices that have facilitated my growth, I might still be isolated. I might still be bitter.

Since the beginning days of my transition into Lead Pastor, I have managed to usher in some good despite—or perhaps *because* of—the trauma I endured. With the crash course that was my traumatic experience, I could better understand the stresses plaguing our community, the areas in dire need of support. We needed a full renovation, to tear out the damage and start from the cracks in our foundation. With God providing the blueprint, I worked to address each fissure in the structure, simultaneously addressing the many misunderstandings against my character.

They said, *Pastor Dodd's area of doctoral study is not Biblical. It is based in the secular world. He is using the church's funds for his own personal gain!*

I say, we as followers of Christ cannot live between the pages of a book our whole lives; we must apply the Lord's teachings in the real world. My studies in Christian Community Development, plus the kick in the pants I got from Trauma 101, equipped me with the knowledge I needed to embrace a higher calling to healing both within myself and within my community. As fellow pastor Craig Groeschel says, "When the leader gets better, everyone gets better." It is not selfish to take care of your own needs. It might be one of the least selfish actions you have in your arsenal—to decide that you are not above self-improvement.

I cannot speak of real world applications without offering real world examples. Actions speak louder than words, and claiming to develop a Christian community is nothing without proof. Today, we have partnered with community organizations to bring food, socialization, and education to the neighborhood we call home. Again, I say that the glory and wonder of God exists past the Bible Study door and out into the real world, even if only across the street. Where there is good to be done and pain to be healed, His children must progress past the page, allowing the Word to guide our steps rather than trip us up. The Gospel must hit the pavement, as I like to say, for "...faith by itself, if it is not accompanied by action, is dead" (James 2:17 NIV).

The widespread plight of single motherhood in our community led us to start an afterschool program focused on academic excellence and a summer camp that runs as late as seven p.m. Both of these programs give the gift of time to mothers who need it the most. Whether that be used for grocery shopping or a well-earned nap, our mothers feel supported by their church community. We take care of our seniors, too. Every week, seniors are given a space to socialize with one another and enjoy a healthy snack at the cafe, created specially for the older folks in our neighborhood. Most importantly, no one has to be a member of our church to feel loved and accepted within our walls.

They said, *Pastor Dodd fails to put God and His children first. He cannot possibly be a successful pastor with a bi-vocational life distracting him from his divine calling.*

I say, being a pastor is bi-vocational. It is being a student and a teacher of the Word of God. It is being a motivational speaker. It is being a community planner, a project manager, a chief fundraiser, a counselor, a coach, an overall hype-man for the congregation.

Simultaneously completing my studies and leading a small congregation of my own only prepared me for the complexities of becoming Lead Pastor of an established church community. But then they went as far as to say, *Pastor Dodd lacks the "leadership material" of his predecessor.* That one hurt.

For a while, I did not have a response to those words. But today, after years of educating myself, reflecting on my leadership style, and respecting the process of healing, I say this: The criteria for good leadership is more nuanced than a one-to-one comparison. I will not shy away from my faults, but I will also not discredit my strengths. After all, where I am weak, I seek the counsel of the strong. I am blessed to have a team of unique individuals in my corner who share my vision. They can see around the opposing corner, past the negative opinions and obstructions that would block a less creative mind's view, into the future that I wish for this community.

No leader has a one hundred percent approval rating, and I have certainly lost people along the way. That will happen, no matter your good intentions. Even so, the response of the community at large has been overwhelmingly positive. For the first time in this church's history, people unaffiliated with the church are engaging in a meaningful way. They can feel the deep-rooted connection between our church and the village we serve. They recognize the redirection of our mission, the rectification of past disparities when mission work overseas was more prevalent than mission work in our own backyard.

What, between all this back and forth, does God have to say? Let us review the words He spoke to a young leader in one of my favorite books of the Bible, Joshua 1:2-9 NIV:

"Moses my servant is dead. Now then, you and all these people, get ready to cross the Jordan River into the land I am about to give to them—to the Israelites. I will give you every place where you set your foot, as I promised Moses. Your territory will extend from the desert to Lebanon, and from the great river, the Euphrates—all the Hittite country—to the Mediterranean Sea in the west. No one will be able to stand against you all the days of your life. As I was with Moses, so I will be with you; I will never leave you nor forsake you. Be strong and courageous, because you will lead these people to inherit the land I swore to their ancestors to give them.

Be strong and very courageous. Be careful to obey all the law my servant Moses gave you; do not turn from it to the right or to the left, that you may be successful wherever you go. Keep this Book of the Law always on your lips; meditate on it day and night, so that you may be careful to do everything written in it. Then you will be prosperous and successful. Have I not commanded you? Be strong and courageous. Do not be afraid; do not be discouraged, for the Lord your God will be with you wherever you go."

"Be strong and courageous." God speaks these words to Joshua three times. If you are to take anything away from this passage, that is it. Criticisms may damage your ego, but there is nothing more leader-like than being strong and being courageous in God's eyes. Who else's eyes are more important than our Father's?

Are We There Yet?

I hope you have learned something from this book, whether it be a new perspective on your own trauma or an affirmation of your approach to leadership. Writing this book with the support of my family, friends, and colleagues has immensely contributed to my own healing journey. *The Trauma in Transition* is not just a catchy title. It captures an unforgettable time in my life when I wished I had a guidebook to tell me how to navigate the hardships I endured—the same guidebook that I can now offer to others.

This final page may leave you without all of the answers you seek. You may very well continue to feel isolated and bitter, caught up in the painful vortex of misunderstanding. If the bridge over these troubled waters is not immediately clear to you, take comfort in the fact that it rarely is so easy. 2 Corinthians 4:7-10 NIV reminds us that God is right there with us through it all:

> "But we have this treasure in jars of clay to show that this all-surpassing power is from God and not from us. We are hard pressed on every side, but not crushed; perplexed, but not in despair; persecuted, but not abandoned; struck down, but not destroyed. We always carry around in our body the death of Jesus, so that the life of Jesus may also be revealed in our body."

One more time: "Hard pressed, but not crushed. Perplexed, but not in despair. Persecuted, but not abandoned. Struck down, but not destroyed." In life, we will endure trauma and all of its pressures, uncertainties, fights, and wounds. But never, *never* will we be alone on the journey, no matter how long or far we have left to go.

I remember being a child, traveling with my parents to visit my grandparents in Mississippi. I would stare out the window of our Cadillac Seville, listen to the music on the radio, and count the mile markers. Not even ten miles out of Chicago, I would begin to ask, "Are we there yet?" and catch my mother's reflection in the rearview mirror, her familiar eyes looking back at me. "Not yet," she would say. I would ask again and again, until my parents would no longer respond, as tired of the journey as I was. For the rest of the drive, I would have to trust that with time, distance, and God's providence, we would eventually reach our destination. And every time, we did.

These days, there are no more long road trips with my parents. Now, I am the one at the wheel and my children are the impatient passengers. But there is not a day that goes by that I do not remember their lessons, their strength, and their love of God. It is said that you are born looking like your parents, but die looking like your decisions. As I age with each passing year, I still have my mother's eyes and my father's smile. Above all, I like to think that I also have their blessing.

As you navigate the trauma in transition, embarking on your own healing journey through the unknown, I hope you know that you have mine.

1. Describe the trauma that has paralyzed your forward momentum. Upon completing this book, what steps will you take to jumpstart your healing journey?

2. It has been said that you cannot conquer what you will not confront. What must you confront? How will this confrontation bring you closer to God's vision for your life?

3. Philippians 4:13 NIV states, "I can do all this through Him who gives me strength." I believe you have the God-given ability to triumph over trauma. Envision how you want the end of your story to read. Are you an author like me? A visionary? A world mover and shaker?

Notes

Introduction

1. "Revelation 3 NIV." *Bible Hub*, Biblica, Inc., biblehub.com/niv/revelation/3.htm. Accessed 30 Sep. 2021.

Chapter 1 — *The Pain in Transition*

2. Tureaud, Lawrence (Mr. T), actor. *Rocky III*. MGM/UA Entertainment Co., 1982.
3. Roosevelt, Franklin D. "Quote by Franklin D. Roosevelt." *Goodreads*. Goodreads, Inc., goodreads.com/quotes/1324527-a-smooth-sea-never-made-a-skilled-sailor. Accessed 30 Sep. 2021
4. Berardino, Mark. "Mike Tyson explains one of his most famous quotes." *South Florida Sun Sentinel*, Sun Sentinel, 12 Nov. 2012, sun-sentinel.com/sports/fl-xpm-2012-11-09-sfl-mike-tyson-explains-one-of-his-most-famous-quotes-20121109-story.html. Accessed 30 Sep. 2021.
5. Washington, Denzel, actor. *The Equalizer 2*. Sony Pictures Releasing, 2018.
6. "Genesis 37 NIV." *Bible Hub*, Biblica, Inc., biblehub.com/niv/genesis/37.htm. Accessed 30 Sep. 2021.
7. Hartney, Dr. Elizabeth. "How Emotional Pain Addiction Causes Physical Issues." *Verywell Mind*, Dotdash, 7 July 2020, verywellmind.com/physical-pain-and-emotional-pain-22421. Accessed 30 Sep. 2021.
8. "Psalm 13 NIV." *Bible Hub*, Biblica, Inc., biblehub.com/niv/psalms/13.htm. Accessed 30 Sep. 2021.
9. "Matthew 27 NIV." *Bible Hub*, Biblica, Inc., biblehub.com/niv/matthew/27.htm. Accessed 30 Sep. 2021.
10. Boyz II Men. "It's So Hard To Say Goodbye To Yesterday." *Cooleyhighharmony*, Motown, 1975. *Spotify*,

open.spotify.com/track/264JdkdtNRAGL4M4PnDYHC?si
=bl7vqW45TRGvutaQD0hlnQ.

11. "A Great War Leaves the Country with Three..."
Quotery.com, Quotery, quotery.com/quotes/great-war-leaves-country-three. Accessed 30 Sep. 2021.

12. Rath, Tom, and Donald O. Clifton. "The Power of Praise and Recognition." *Gallup*, Gallup, Inc., 20 Oct. 2020, news.gallup.com/businessjournal/12157/power-praise-recognition.aspx. Accessed 30 Sep. 2021.

Chapter 2 — *The Pieces of the Puzzle*

13. Briggs Myers, Isabel. "The 16 MBTI® Types." *The Myers & Briggs Foundation*, The Myers & Briggs Foundation, myersbriggs.org/my-mbti-personality-type/mbti-basics/the-16-mbti-types.htm. Accessed 30 Sep. 2021.

14. "MBTI® Basics." *The Myers & Briggs Foundation*, The Myers & Briggs Foundation, myersbriggs.org/my-mbti-personality-type/mbti-basics. Accessed Sep. 2021.

15. "1 Samuel 17 NIV." *Bible Hub*, Biblica, Inc., biblehub.com/niv/1_samuel/17.htm. Accessed 30 Sep. 2021.

16. "Matthew 9 NIV." *Bible Hub*, Biblica, Inc., biblehub.com/niv/matthew/9.htm. Accessed 30 Sep. 2021.

17. "Be yourself; everyone else is taken. - Oscar Wilde." *Forbes Quotes*, Forbes.com LLC, forbes.com/quotes/11441. Accessed 30 Sep. 2021.

18. "If you want to go fast go alone. If you want to go far go together. - African Proverb." *Quotespedia*, quotespedia.org, quotespedia.org/authors/a/african-proverbs/if-you-want-to-go-fast-go-alone-if-you-want-to-go-far-go-together-african-proverb. Accessed 30 Sep. 2021.

19. Confucius. "A Quote by Confucius." *Goodreads*, Goodreads Inc., goodreads.com/quotes/7854941-if-you-are-the-smartest-person-in-the-room-then. Accessed 30 Sep. 2021.

20. "i Style." *Discprofile.com*, Everything DiSC, discprofile.com/what-is-disc/disc-styles/influence. Accessed 30 Sep. 2021.

21. Walker, Dr. Joseph W. *Leadership and Loneliness*, Joseph W. Walker III, 2020, p. 52.

22. Mandela, Nelson. *Nelson Mandela By Himself: The Authorised Book of Quotations*, MacMillan, 2011, p. 217.

23. Waldo Emerson, Ralph. "Self-reliance." *Essays*, James Munroe and Company, 1841, p. 47. *Wikisource*, en.wikisource.org/wiki/Page:Essays_(1841).djvu/59. Accessed 30 Sep. 2021.

24. Griffin, Thomas. "Mission Statement vs. Vision Statement: What's the Difference?" *Thomas Griffin*, Griffin Media LLC, 13 Nov. 2020, thomasgriffin.com/mission-statement-vs-vision-statement. Accessed 30 Sep. 2021.

25. "Mark 4 NIV." *Bible Hub*, Biblica, Inc., biblehub.com/niv/mark/4.htm. Accessed 30 Sep. 2021.

26. "Proverbs 3 NIV." *Bible Hub*, Biblica, Inc., biblehub.com/niv/proverbs/3.htm. Accessed 30 Sep. 2021.

Chapter 3 — *Partnerships for Progress*

27. "1 Kings 19 NIV." *Bible Hub*, Biblica, Inc., biblehub.com/niv/1_kings/19.htm. Accessed 30 Sep. 2021.

28. "1 Samuel 18 NIV." *Bible Hub*, Biblica, Inc., biblehub.com/niv/1_samuel/18.htm. Accessed 30 Sep. 2021.

29. "1 Samuel 20 NIV." *Bible Hub*, Biblica, Inc., biblehub.com/niv/1_samuel/20.htm. Accessed 30 Sep. 2021.

30. "Proverbs 13 NIV." *Bible Hub*, Biblica, Inc., biblehub.com/niv/proverbs/13.htm. Accessed 30 Sep. 2021.

31. Whodini. "Friends." *Escape*, Jive Records, 1984. *Spotify*. open.spotify.com/track/3e8KC0EoBmKGuD5LwBvj4U?si =fSHlAOs4TPmW-6ZR1JkMeQ. Accessed 30 Sep. 2021.

Chapter 4 — *Practices for Progress*

32. "Burnout." *Psychology Today*, Sussex Publishers, LLC, psychologytoday.com/us/basics/burnout. Accessed 30 Sep. 2021.

33. Crosswalk Editorial Staff. "The Lord's Prayer - Our Father Who Art in Heaven - Bible Verses & Meaning." *Crosswalk.com*, Salem Media Group, crosswalk.com/faith/prayer/the-lords-prayer-be-encouraged-and-strengthened.html. Accessed 30 Sep. 2021.

34. "Mark 12 NIV." *Bible Hub*, Biblica, Inc., biblehub.com/niv/mark/12.htm. Accessed 30 Sep. 2021.

35. Doran, George T. "There's a S.M.A.R.T. way to write management's goals and objectives." *Management Review*, Vol. 70, Issue 11, pp. 35-36, community.mis.temple.edu/mis0855002fall2015/files/2015/10/S.M.A.R.T-Way-Management-Review.pdf. Accessed 30 Sep. 2021.

36. MrandMrsMuscle. *YouTube*, joined 17 Jan. 2016, https://www.youtube.com/channel/UCi_J6WNj99ro-9cPZOUrf8Q.

Chapter 5 — *Progressing Past Pain*

37. "James 2 NIV." *Bible Hub*, Biblica, Inc., biblehub.com/niv/james/2.htm. Accessed 30 Sep. 2021.

38. "Joshua 1 NIV." *Bible Hub*, Biblica, Inc., biblehub.com/niv/joshua/1.htm. Accessed 30 Sep. 2021.

39. "2 Corinthians 4 NIV." *Bible Hub*, Biblica, Inc., biblehub.com/niv/2_corinthians/4.htm. Accessed 30 Sep. 2021.

40. "Philippians 4 NIV." *Bible Hub*, Biblica, Inc., biblehub.com/niv/philippians/4.htm. Accessed 30 Sep. 2021.

Words of Praise for
The Trauma in Transition

"Transitions and revitalizations can be brutal and are not for the faint of heart. Reading *The Trauma in Transition* reminded me of my own bruising in pastoral ministry, and that we all have a choice to make as leaders who have experienced trauma. We can either use the trauma to make us better, or we can become bitter. I can attest that my friend Dr. Dodd has become better! The lessons and principles he shares are important for anyone wanting to revitalize a church or business of any kind."

- Rev. Bryan Moak, Vice President of Church Strengthening, Converge MidAmerica

"Chris Dodd, in this revealing and transparent offering, demonstrates the power of personal testimony and the passionate skill of storytelling. He comes to us in the spirit of Christ to reveal the truth of his own trauma and the resulting transformation he experienced. The knowledge of his own truth contributed to his freedom, and as his truth is read and considered by others it will contribute to their freedom—"…the truth will give you freedom…" John 8:32. I celebrate Chris and this incredible contribution to the world and the church.

- Dr. Gerald M. Dew, Director of Southside Center for Urban Leadership, Affiliate Professor of Ministry at Northern Seminary

"Dr. Christopher Dodd is a gifted storyteller and offers some great insights and tools for navigating through traumatic transitions. As a friend, I witnessed firsthand the challenges, slander, and attacks he and his family endured. The good news is—by the grace of God—they did endure. This book is one that everyone, especially leaders, should have as a resource while navigating through the transitions of life."

-   Pastor James L. Brooks, Senior Pastor of Harmony Church, Vice-President of Mission & Community at Lawndale Christian Health

"This book does a great job of giving pastors the tools to overcome the pain and mental anguish that comes with leading a rebellious church, and to understand that God uses trauma for leaders to further develop their spiritual, mental, and emotional toughness."

-   Andrew D. Singleton, Jr., Senior Pastor of Victory Apostolic Church

"*The Trauma in Transition* is a ministry of healing for pastors who have experienced the awfulness of leadership trauma. Dr. Dodd has done a phenomenal job articulating the leadership wounds and providing practical leadership principles of healing in addressing this trauma. This book is a necessary read for all pastors and leaders of God's people."

-   Dr. Chad E. Rankin, Founder/Senior Pastor of House of Hope Church

Want to share your own testimony? Respond to *The Trauma in Transition* and tell us your story at drchrisdodd.com